LIFE CYCLES

The
Mountain Lion

Published by Raintree Steck-Vaughn Publishers, an imprint of Steck-Vaughn Company.

Acknowledgments
Project Editor: Pam Wells
Design Manager: Joyce Spicer
Editor: Sabrina Crewe
Designers: Ian Winton and Steve Prosser
Consultant: Michael Chinery
Illustrator: Robert Morton
Electronic Cover Production: Alan Klemp
Additional Electronic Production: Scott Melcer
Photography credits on page 32

Planned and produced by The Creative Publishing Company

Library of Congress Cataloging-in-Publication Data
Crewe, Sabrina
   The mountain lion / Sabrina Crewe ; [illustrator, Robert Morton].
      p.   cm. — (Life cycles)
   Includes index.
   Summary: Describes the physical characteristics, behavior, and life cycle of the puma.
   ISBN 0-8172-4378-X (hardcover) — ISBN 0-8172-6239-3 (pbk.)
   1. Pumas — Juvenile literature.   2. Pumas — Life cycles — Juvenile literature.
   [1. Pumas.]   I. Morton, Robert, ill. II. Title.   III. Series: Crewe, Sabrina. Life cycles.
   QL737.C23C69 1998
   599.75'24 — dc21   96-53251
                                                                 CIP   AC

   2 3 4 5 6 7 8 9 0 LB 01 00 99 98 97
Printed and bound in the United States of America.

Words explained in the glossary appear in **bold** the first time they are used in the text.

LIFE CYCLES

The
Mountain Lion

Sabrina Crewe

RSVP

RAINTREE
STECK-VAUGHN
PUBLISHERS
The Steck-Vaughn Company

Austin, Texas

The mountain lion has two new cubs.

The mountain lion has made a **den** in a cave. She has lined the den with moss and other plants. Two cubs have been born in the den. At first their eyes are closed. The cubs feed on their mother's milk.

The cubs peek out of the den.

The cubs are three weeks old. Their eyes
have opened, and they can move around
in the den. Their mother goes out to hunt
during the day and evening. At night she
nurses the cubs and keeps them warm.

The cub is out of the den.

When the cubs are a few weeks old, they start to go outside their den. The cub's spots help to **camouflage** it, but it is still in danger from **predators**. If a cub goes too far, its mother will catch it gently in her mouth.

The mountain lion brings some food.

The mother mountain lion has caught a
trout. She takes it back to the den to share
with her cubs. The cubs are six weeks
old. Their mother still feeds them with
milk, but now they can eat meat, too.

The cubs are playing.

As the cubs get bigger, they spend more time outside the den. Their mother watches them while they play. The cubs' games are very important. They are learning **skills** that they will need as adults.

The cubs learn new skills.

The cubs practice **stalking** and catching food. They do this by chasing each other or by pouncing on sticks. They also learn to climb trees to escape from danger.

The cubs learn from their mother.

Now the cubs are a few months old. They can go farther from the den. When their mother goes hunting, they follow her.

The cub meets a badger.

As cubs get bigger, their spots begin to fade. The cub is still too young to hunt. It is learning about different kinds of **prey**. Mountain lions hunt badgers, porcupines, and other animals. They hunt and eat deer most often.

The cub is eight months old.

By winter, the cubs have grown much bigger. Their spots have all gone. The cubs still hunt with their mother, but now they start to catch their own prey. The mountain lions sleep in dens during winter and keep each other warm.

The mountain lion hunts on its own.

The winter is over. By now the young mountain lion has learned to hunt for itself. It will stay with its mother for only a few more months.

The mountain lions have left their mother.

Young mountain lions leave their mothers after they are one year old. They are ready to take care of themselves. The young mountain lions stay together for a few more months while they explore new areas.

The mountain lion lives by itself.

The mountain lion looks for a **home range** where it can live alone. It needs an area where it can make safe dens. It needs places to hunt and find water.

The mountain lion scratches a tree.

The mountain lion has chosen a home range.
It makes its mark on a tree trunk. Now other
animals will know it lives there. Other
mountain lions may share parts of its home
range, but they stay away from each other.

The mountain lion has a winter range.

In winter, herds of deer come down from the mountains to **graze** where there is less snow. The mountain lion follows the deer to the lower ground. If it lives near the deer in winter, it will be able to hunt them for food.

The mountain lion is stalking.

The mountain lion has found a herd of deer.
It creeps forward slowly. The mountain lion
stays low to the ground, hidden by the snow.
The mountain lion needs to get close before
it starts to chase the deer.

The mountain lion chases its prey.

The mountain lion can run very fast, but only for a short distance. It chases an old deer because that one will be easier to catch. When the mountain lion reaches the deer, it jumps on the deer's back.

The mountain lion has killed the deer.

Mountain lions use their teeth and claws to kill their prey. When the deer is dead, the mountain lion drags it to a safe place. It eats as much as it can.

The mountain lion has eaten a good meal.

When the mountain lion is full, it covers the deer with branches and leaves. This helps hide the body from other hungry animals. The mountain lion will come back to eat until the meat is all gone. After about a week, it will go hunting again.

Another mountain lion comes near.

Male mountain lions travel over larger areas than females. A male has come into the home range of the female. The female does not let him come close to her at first. When she is sure he will not attack her, she lets him stay.

The mountain lion has a mate.

The mountain lions stay together for about two weeks. They hunt together and sleep in the same places. Mountain lions only spend time together when they are ready to mate. Three months after mating, the female mountain lion will give birth to her cubs.

Mountain lions need to be by themselves.

Mountain lions cannot live where there are people. Even though they rarely hurt people, mountain lions are killed by farmers because they may eat cattle and sheep. People can help mountain lions by protecting **wilderness** areas where they can live.

Parts of a Mountain Lion

Mountain lions and other cats belong to a group of **mammals** called **carnivores**. Like other mammals, carnivores have fur and feed their young with milk. All carnivores are hunters, with sharp claws and teeth. Cats eat only meat.

Fur
Grows thicker in winter
Color helps animal to blend in
with background

Legs
Very powerful for running,
jumping, and climbing

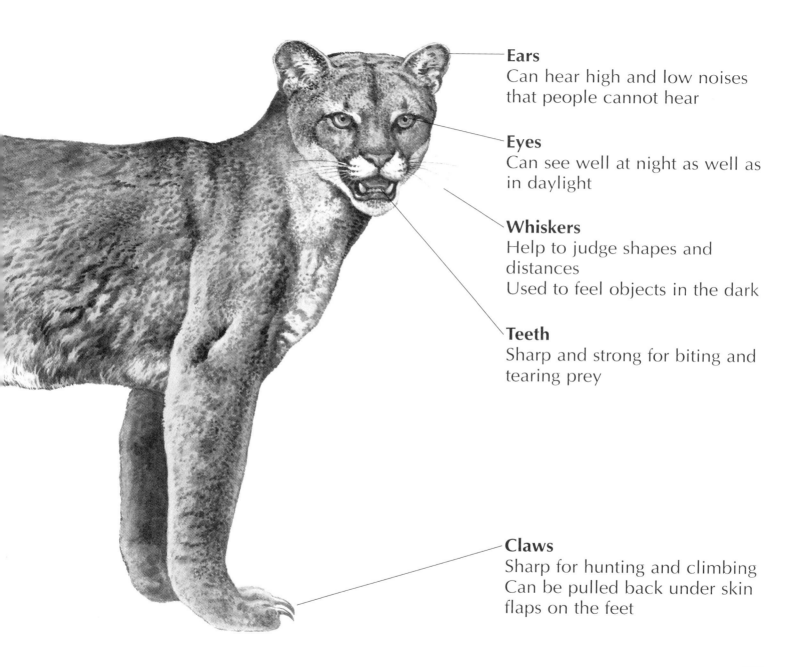

Ears
Can hear high and low noises that people cannot hear

Eyes
Can see well at night as well as in daylight

Whiskers
Help to judge shapes and distances
Used to feel objects in the dark

Teeth
Sharp and strong for biting and tearing prey

Claws
Sharp for hunting and climbing
Can be pulled back under skin flaps on the feet

Other Cats

A mountain lion has other names. It is also called a puma, a cougar, and a panther. The mountain lion is the largest member of a group called small cats. Here are some other small cats and some large cats, too. All cats live in the wild except for domestic cats, which are kept as pets.

Domestic cat

SMALL CATS

Lynx

Indian desert cat

Leopard

Lion

LARGE CATS

Jaguar

Tiger

29

Where the Mountain Lion Lives

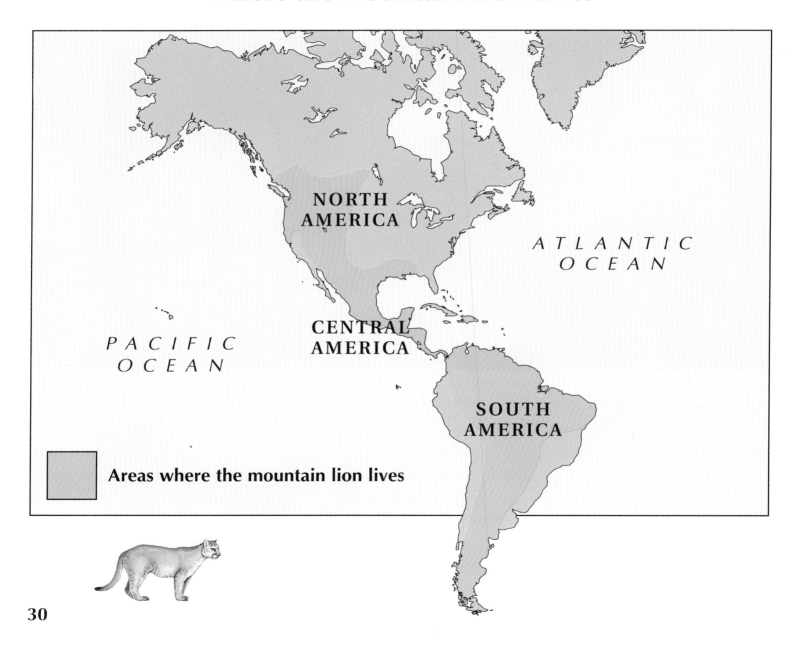

NORTH
AMERICA

ATLANTIC
OCEAN

PACIFIC
OCEAN

CENTRAL
AMERICA

SOUTH
AMERICA

Areas where the mountain lion lives

Glossary

Camouflage A way of hiding something against its background

Carnivore A type of animal that eats meat

Den The place where a wild animal lives or has its young

Graze To feed on growing grass

Home range The area in which an animal lives its day-to-day life

Mammal A kind of animal that usually has fur and feeds its young with milk

Nurse To feed young animals with mother's milk

Predator An animal that hunts and kills other animals for food

Prey An animal hunted or killed by another animal for food

Skill The ability to do something well

Stalking Following or approaching prey while staying hidden

Wilderness A place where people have not lived, built, or farmed

Index

Camouflage **6**
Carnivores **26**
Cubs **4–12, 23**
Deer **11, 17–21**
Den **4–8, 10, 12, 15**
Food **7, 9, 17**
Home range **15, 16, 22**
Hunting **10, 11, 12, 13, 15, 17, 18–19, 21, 23**
Mammals **26**
Mating **23**
Milk **4, 7, 26**
Predators **6**
Prey **11, 20**
Skills **8, 9**
Stalking **9, 18**
Trout **7**
Wilderness **24**
Winter **12, 13, 17**

Photography credits

Life Cycles introduces young readers to the lives of animals in the wild. The simple text and colorful photos and illustrations encourage young children to read and enjoy these books on their own.

Titles in the series

The Alligator	The Chimpanzee	The Prairie Dog
The Bear	The Frog	The Salmon
The Beaver	The Kangaroo	The Snake
The Bee	The Ladybug	The Spider
The Buffalo	The Mountain Lion	The Swallow
The Butterfly	The Penguin	The Whale

RSVP®
RAINTREE
STECK-VAUGHN
P U B L I S H E R S
The Steck-Vaughn Company

ISBN 0-8172-6239-3

90000

9 780817 262396